C000218105

German Dialogues for Beginners

Book 4

Over 100 Daily Used Phrases and Short Stories to Learn German in Your Car. Have Fun and Grow Your Vocabulary with Crazy Effective Language Learning Lessons

www.LearnLikeNatives.com

© **Copyright 2020**

By Learn Like A Native

TABLE OF CONTENT

INTRODUCTION

Before we dive into some German, I want to congratulate you, whether you're just beginning, continuing, or resuming your language learning journey. Here at Learn Like a Native, we understand the determination it takes to pick up a new language and after reading this book, you'll be another step closer to achieving your language goals.

As a thank you for learning with us, we are giving you free access to our 'Speak Like a Native' eBook. It's packed full of practical advice and insider tips on how to make language learning quick, easy, and most importantly, enjoyable. Head over to LearnLikeNatives.com to access your free guide and peruse our huge selection of language learning resources.

Learning a new language is a bit like cooking—you need several different ingredients and the right technique, but the end result is sure to be delicious. We created this book of short stories for learning German because language is alive. Language is about the senses—hearing, tasting the words on your tongue, and touching another culture up close. Learning a language in a classroom is a fine place to start, but it's not a complete introduction to a language.

In this book, you'll find a language come to life. These short stories are miniature immersions into the German language, at a level that is perfect for beginners. This book is not a lecture on grammar. It's not an endless vocabulary list. This book is the closest you can come to a language immersion without leaving the country. In the stories within, you will see people speaking to each other, going through daily life situations, and using the most common, helpful words and phrases in language.

You are holding the key to bringing your German studies to life.

Made for Beginners

We made this book with beginners in mind. You'll find that the language is simple, but not boring. Most of the book is in the present tense, so you will be able to focus on dialogues, root verbs, and understand and find patterns in subject-verb agreement.

This is not "just" a translated book. While reading novels and short stories translated into German is a wonderful thing, beginners (and even novices) often run into difficulty. Literary licenses and complex sentence structure can make reading in your second language truly difficult—not to mention BORING. That's why German Short Stories for Beginners is the perfect book to pick up. The stories are simple, but not infantile. They were not written for children, but the language is simple so that beginners can pick it up.

The Benefits of Learning a Second Language

If you have picked up this book, it's likely that you are already aware of the many benefits of learning a second language. Besides just being fun, knowing more than one language opens up a whole new world to you. You will be able to communicate with a much larger chunk of the world. Opportunities in the workforce will open up, and maybe even your day-to-day work will be improved. Improved communication can also help you expand your business. And from a neurological perspective, learning a second language is like taking your daily vitamins and eating well, for your brain!

How To Use The Book

The chapters of this book all follow the same structure:

- A short story with several dialogs
- A summary in German
- A list of important words and phrases and their English translation
- Questions to test your understanding
- Answers to check if you were right
- The English translation of the story to clear every doubt

You may use this book however is comfortable for you, but we have a few recommendations for getting the most out of the experience. Try these tips and if they work for you, you can use them on every chapter throughout the book.

1) Start by reading the story all the way through. Don't stop or get hung up on any particular words or phrases. See how much of the plot you can understand in this way. We think you'll get a lot more of it than you may expect, but it is completely normal not to understand everything in the story. You are learning a new language, and that takes time.

2) Read the summary in German. See if it matches what you have understood of the plot.

3) Read the story through again, slower this time. See if you can pick up the meaning of any words or phrases you don't understand by using context clues and the information from the summary.

4) Test yourself! Try to answer the five comprehension questions that come at the end of each story. Write your answers

down, and then check them against the answer key. How did you do? If you didn't get them all, no worries!

5) Look over the vocabulary list that accompanies the chapter. Are any of these the words you did not understand? Did you already know the meaning of some of them from your reading?

6) Now go through the story once more. Pay attention this time to the words and phrases you haven't understand. If you'd like, take the time to look them up to expand your meaning of the story. Every time you read over the story, you'll understand more and more.

7) Move on to the next chapter when you are ready.

Read and Listen

The audio version is the best way to experience this book, as you will hear a native German speaker tell you each story. You will become accustomed to their accent as you listen along, a huge plus for when you want to apply your new language skills in the real world.

If this has ignited your language learning passion and you are keen to find out what other resources are available, go to LearnLikeNatives.com, where you can access our vast range of free learning materials. Don't know where to begin? An excellent place to start is our 'Speak Like a Native' free eBook, full of practical advice and insider tips on how to make language learning quick, easy, and most importantly, enjoyable.

And remember, small steps add up to great advancements! No moment is better to begin learning than the present.

FREE BOOK!

Get the *FREE BOOK* that reveals the secrets path to learn any language fast, and without leaving your country.

Discover:

- The **language 5 golden rules** to master languages at will

- Proven **mind training techniques** to revolutionize your learning

- A complete step-by-step guide to **conquering any language**

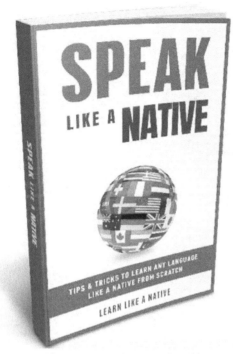

CHAPTER 1
The Driver's License / question words

HANDLUNG

Wayne lebt in einer Stadt. Wayne ist vierzig Jahre alt. Normalerweise fährt er mit seinem Auto zur Arbeit. Wayne kommt heute zu spät zur Arbeit. Wayne fährt immer schneller. Er fährt über dem Tempolimit. Er muss pünktlich zur Arbeit. Heute hat er ein wichtiges Treffen.

Wayne hört ein Geräusch. Er schaut hinter sich. Hinter ihm ist ein Polizeiauto. Oh, nein, denkt er sich. Ich fahre ziemlich schnell. Er hält das Auto an. Der Polizeiwagen hält auch an. Ein Polizist steigt aus. Er geht zu Waynes Auto.

"Hallo", sagt der Polizist.

"Hallo, Herr Wachmeister", sagt Wayne.

"**Warum** habe ich Sie wohl angehalten?" fragt der Polizist.

"Ich weiß nicht, **welches** Gesetz breche ich?" fragt Wayne.

"Sie fahren viel zu schnell", sagt der Polizist.

"**Wie viele** Stundenkilometer bin ich über dem Tempolimit?" fragt Wayne.

"Genug", sagt der Polizist. "**Wo** wollen Sie denn so eilig hin?"

"Zur Arbeit", sagt Wayne.

"Zeigen Sie mir Ihren Führerschein", sagt der Polizist. Wayne holt seine Brieftasche raus. Er öffnet sie. Er zieht seinen Führerschein raus. Er gibt ihn dem Polizisten.

"Der ist abgelaufen", sagt der Polizist. "Sie stecken in großen Schwierigkeiten." Der Polizist sagt Wayne, er könne nicht mit einem abgelaufenen Führerschein fahren. Wayne muss einen neuen Führerschein beantragen. Wayne stimmt zu. Der Polizist sagt ihm, dass er heute nicht zur Arbeit fahren kann. Wayne muss ohne Auto auskommen.

Wayne muss aufhören, sein Auto zu fahren. Jetzt geht er auf andere Weise zur Arbeit. Er kann zwischen dem Zug oder dem Bus wählen. Manchmal fährt er mit dem Fahrrad. Wenn er zu spät kommt, nimmt er ein Taxi. Heute ist er wieder zu spät.

Wayne kommt im Büro an.

"Hallo, Wayne", sagt sein Kollege Xavier, "**wie** bist du hierher gekommen? Dein Führerschein ist abgelaufen, richtig?"

"Ja, das ist er", sagt Wayne. "Heute bin ich mit dem Taxi gekommen. **Wie weit** wohnst du entfernt von hier?" Xavier läuft normalerweise zur Arbeit.

"Ich wohne einen Kilometer entfernt", sagt Xavier. "**Wie lange** braucht ein Taxi, um hierher zu kommen?"

"Hmmm, ungefähr 20 Minuten", sagt Wayne.

"Nicht schlecht", sagt Xavier. "Und **wie viel** kostet das Taxi?"

"Etwa 20 Dollar", sagt Wayne.

"Oh, das ist ein bisschen teuer", sagt Xavier. "Welches Taxiunternehmen ist es?

"Birmingham Taxi", sagt Wayne. "Warum bist du so interessiert?"

"Meiner Familie gehört ein Taxiunternehmen", sagt Xavier. "Mein Bruder leitet es."

"Nett", sagt Wayne. "Kann ich eine Gratisfahrt bekommen?" Beide lachen. Wayne scherzt. Aber er muss sein Problem lösen. Er kann nicht jeden Tag für ein Taxi bezahlen. Er entschließt, dass er sich morgen um seinen Führerschein kümmert.

Am nächsten Tag fährt Wayne mit dem Bus zum Bürgeramt zur Führerscheinstelle. Das ist das Gebäude, wo die Leute ihren Führerschein bekommen. Er steigt aus dem Bus. Die Leute stehen draußen in einer Schlange. Viele Leute wollen ihren Führerschein abholen. Das Büro ist langsam. Er stellt sich in die Schlange. Nach einer Stunde ist er im Gebäude. Es gibt eine weiter Schlange, er wartet.

"**Wer** ist der Nächste?" fragt die Frau.

"Ich", sagt Wayne.

"Na, dann komm mal her!" sagt sie. Sie ist ungeduldig. "**Was** brauchst du?"

"Ich muss meinen Führerschein erneuern", sagt Wayne.

"Gib mir deinen alten Führerschein", sagt sie.

"Ich habe ihn nicht", sagt Wayne. Sie starrt ihn an. Sie scheint wütend zu sein.

"**Warum hast** du ihn **nicht**?" fragt sie.

"Ich kann ihn nicht finden", sagt Wayne.

"**Mit wem** spreche ich?" fragt sie.

"Was meinen Sie damit?" fragt Wayne. Er ist verwirrt.

"Okay, Schlaumeier, sag mir deinen Vor- und Nachnamen", sagt sie. Wayne sagt es ihr.

"**Wie alt** bist du?" fragt sie.

"**Wofür**?" fragt Wayne.

"Ich muss dein Geburtsdatum bestätigen", sagt sie. "**Wann** bist du geboren?"

Wayne sagt es ihr. Sie schaut auf ihren Computer. Sie braucht viel Zeit. Sie schüttelt ihren Kopf.

"Ich kann dich nicht finden", sagt sie. "Es gibt heute ein Problem mit dem System. Komm morgen wieder."

"Ich kann nicht", sagt Wayne.

"Wenn du heute deinen Führerschein willst, musst du die Fahrprüfung machen", sagt sie.

"**Wieso**?" fragt Wayne.

"Der Computer sagt, du hast keinen Führerschein", sagt sie. Wayne braucht heute seinen Führerschein. Er geht zur anderen Reihe. Er macht die Fahrprüfung. Einfach denk er sich. Er weiß, wie man fährt. Alle anderen sind Jugendliche. Er ist der Älteste in der Reihe.

"**Wer** ist dran?" fragt ein großer Mann mit einem braunen Anzug.

"Ich", sagt Wayne. Er folgt dem großen Mann zum Auto. Sie steigen ins Auto. Wayne versucht sich an alles zu erinnern, was man bei einer Fahrprüfung macht. Er kontrolliert die Spiegel. Er legt den Sicherheitsgurt an. Er sieht, wie der Prüfer auf einen Merkzettel schreibt.

"Okay, los gehts", sagt der Prüfer.

Wayne fährt vorsichtig rückwärts aus der Parklücke. Er fährt langsam. Er benutzt seinen Blinker. Er begibt sich auf die Straße und fährt unter dem Tempolimit. Der Prüfer leitet ihn durch die Stadt. Wayne achtet darauf, an gelben Ampeln anzuhalten und den Blinker zu benutzen. Wayne macht gute Arbeit.

Wayne denkt, dass er besteht. Der Prüfer leitet ihn zurück zur Führerscheinstelle. Der Prüfer weist ihn an, zu stoppen.

"Jetzt müssen Sie seitlich einparken", sagt der Prüfer. Wayne parkt nie seitlich ein. Er ist nervös. Der Prüfer führt ihn zu einem winzigen Parkplatz. Wayne quetscht das Auto in die Parklücke. Er ist fast fertig mit dem Parken, aber dann hört er einen blechernen Ton. Er rammt das Auto hinter sich.

"Oh, nein", sagt Wayne.

"Damit sind sie direkt durchgefallen", sagt der Prüfer. "Tut mir leid, Sie haben die Fahrprüfung nicht bestanden."

Wayne steigt aus dem Auto, damit der Prüfer das Auto zurück fahren kann.

"Seit wie vielen Jahren fahren Sie schon Auto?" fragt der Prüfer.

"vierundzwanzig", sagt Wayne. Er schämt sich. Er muss morgen wiederkommen.

ZUSAMMENFASSUNG

Wayne hat einen Führerschein. Er ist abgelaufen, Wayne muss Taxis, Busse und andere Verkehrsmittel nutzen. Er beschließt, seinen Führerschein zu verlängern. Er geht zur Führerscheinstelle, um es zu tun. Er wartet in einer langen Schlange und muss viele Fragen beantworten. Es gibt ein Problem mit dem Computersystem. Wayne muss die Fahrprüfung machen. Er macht einen guten Job mit dem Prüfer im Auto. Allerdings fällt Wayne bei seinem Test durch, weil er das seitliche Einparken nicht geübt hat.

VOKABELLISTE

warum	why
welche	which
wie viele	how many

wo	where
wie	how
wie weit	how far
wie lange	how long
wie viel	how much
wer	who
was	what
warum nicht	why don't
mit wem	with whom
wie alt	how old
wofür	what for
wann	when
wieso	how come
wer/wessen	whose
wie viele	how many

FRAGEN

1) Warum wird Wayne vom Polizisten angehalten?

   a) er fährt über eine rote Ampel

   b) sein Auto ist kaputt

   c) er fährt zu schnell

   d) er ist ein Krimineller

2) Wayne bekommt großen Ärger mit dem Polizisten, weil ...

   a) sein Führerschein abgelaufen ist

   b) sein Auto nicht zugelassen ist

   c) er auf den Polizisten spuckt

   d) er dem Polizeibeamten nicht antwortet

3) Welches davon kostet Wayne 20 Dollar, um zur Arbeit zu kommen?

a) Fahrrad

b) Bus

c) Zug

d) Taxi

4) Wayne taucht nicht im Computersystem der Führerscheinstelle auf. Warum?

a) er hatte nie einen Führerschein

b) er hat einen schlechten Tag

c) es gibt ein Problem mit dem System

d) sein Geburtsdatum ist falsch

.

5) Warum hat Wayne seinen Test nicht bestanden?

a) er ist ein unerfahrener Autofahrer

b) er parkt schlecht, weil er die Art des Parkens nicht benutzt hat

c) er parkt schlecht, weil das Auto zu groß ist

d) er betrunken ist

ANTWORTEN

1) Warum wird Wayne vom Polizisten angehalten?

c) er fährt zu schnell

2) Wayne bekommt großen Ärger mit dem Politisten, weil ...

a) sein Führerschein abgelaufen ist

3) Welches davon kostet Wayne 20 Dollar, um zur Arbeit zu kommen?

d) Taxi

4) Wayne taucht nicht im Computersystem der Führerscheinstelle auf.   Warum?

c) es gibt ein Problem mit dem System

5) Warum hat Wayne seinen Test nicht bestanden?

b) er parkt schlecht, weil er die Art des Parkens nicht benutzt hat

Translation of the Story

The Driver's License

STORY

Wayne lives in a city. Wayne is forty years old. He usually drives his car to work. Wayne is late to work today. Wayne drives faster and faster. He drives over the speed limit. He needs to get to work on time. Today he has an important meeting.

Wayne hears a sound. He looks behind him. There is a police car behind him. Oh, no, he thinks. I am going rather fast. He stops the car. The police car stops, too. A policeman gets out. He walks over to Wayne's car.

"Hello," says the police officer.

"Hello, sir," says Wayne.

"**Why** do you think I pulled you over?" asks the policeman.

"I don't know. **Which** law am I breaking?" asks Wayne.

"You are going way too fast," says the policeman.

"**How many** kilometers per hour am I over the speed limit?" asks Wayne.

"Enough," says the policeman. "**Where** are you going in such a hurry?"

"To work," says Wayne.

"Show me your driver's license," says the officer. Wayne takes out his wallet. He opens it. He pulls out his driver's license. He gives it to the police officer.

"This is expired," says the officer. "You're in big trouble." The officer tells Wayne he can't drive with an expired license. Wayne must get a new license. Wayne agrees. The officer tells him he can't drive to work today. Wayne must live without a car.

Wayne has to stop driving his car. Now he goes to work other ways. He can choose between the train or the bus. Sometimes, he rides his bike. If he is late, he takes a taxi. Today, he is late again.

Wayne arrives to the office.

"Hi, Wayne," says his colleague, Xavier. "**How** did you get here? Your license is expired, right?"

"Yes, it is," says Wayne. "Today I am in taxi. **How far** is your house from here?" Xavier usually walks to work.

"My house is a kilometer away," says Xavier. "**How long** does a taxi take to get here?"

"Oh, about twenty minutes," says Wayne.

"Not bad," says Xavier. "And **how much** does the taxi cost?"

"About twenty dollars," says Wayne.

"Oh, that is a bit expensive," says Xavier. "Which taxi company is it?

"Birmingham Taxi," says Wayne. "Why are you so interested?"

"My family owns a taxi company," says Xavier. "My brother runs it."

"Nice," says Wayne. "Can I get a free ride?" They both laugh. Wayne is kidding. But he needs to solve his problem. He can't pay for a taxi every day. He decides tomorrow he is going to get his license.

The next day, Wayne takes the bus to the DMV, the Department of Motor Vehicles. This is the building where people get their driver's license. He gets out of his car. There is a line outside. Many people have to get their license. The office is slow. He gets in the line. After an hour, he is inside the building. There is another line. He waits.

"**Who** is next?" asks the woman.

"Me," says Wayne.

"Well, come on!" she says. She is impatient. "**What** do you need?"

"I need to renew my license," says Wayne.

"Give me your old card," she says.

"I don't have it," says Wayne. She stares at him. She seems angry.

"**Why don't** you have it?" she asks.

"I can't find it," says Wayne.

"**With whom** am I speaking?" she asks.

"What do you mean?" asks Wayne. He is confused.

"Ok, smart guy, tell me your first and last name," she says. Wayne tells her.

"**How old** are you?" she asks.

"**What for**?" asks Wayne.

"I have to confirm your birth date," she says. "**When** were you born?"

Wayne tells her. She looks at her computer. She takes a long time. She shakes her head.

"I can't find you," she says. "There is a problem with the system today. Come back tomorrow."

"I can't," says Wayne.

"If you want your license today, you will have to take the driving test over," she says.

"**How come**?" asks Wayne.

"The computer says you have no license," she says. Wayne needs his license today. He goes to the other line. He will take his driver's test. Easy, he thinks. He knows how to drive. All the other people are teenagers. He is the oldest in this line.

"**Whose** turn is it?" asks a big man with a brown suit.

"Mine," says Wayne. He follows the big man to his car. They get in the car. Wayne tries to remember everything you do in a driver's test. He checks the mirrors. He puts on his seatbelt. He sees the examiner writing on a notepad.

"Okay, let's go," says the examiner.

Wayne carefully backs out of the parking space. He drives slowly. He uses his turn signal. He gets on the road and drives under the speed limit. The examiner directs him through the town. Wayne makes sure to stop at yellow lights and to use his blinker. Wayne does a good job.

Wayne thinks he passes. The examiner directs him back to the DMV. However, the examiner tells him to stop.

"Now you must parallel park," says the examiner. Wayne never parallel parks. He is nervous. The examiner directs him to a tiny parking space. Wayne turns the car into the space. He is almost finished parking. But then he hears a 'ding' sound. His car hits the car behind him.

"Oh, no," says Wayne.

"That is an automatic fail," says the examiner. "Sorry, you fail your driver's test."

Wayne gets out of the car to let the examiner drive the car back to the office.

"How many years have you been driving?" asks the examiner.

"Twenty-four," says Wayne. He is ashamed. He has to come back tomorrow.

CHAPTER 2
At the Travel Agency / likes and dislikes

HANDLUNG

Yolanda und Zelda sind Schwestern. Sie sind sehr beschäftigt. Sie leben beide in New York City. Yolanda ist eine Friseurin für Prominente. Zelda ist Anwältin und hat zwei Kinder. Sie sind so beschäftigt, dass sie sich manchmal monatelang nicht sehen.

Yolanda hat eines Tages eine Idee. Sie ruft Zelda an.

"Zelda, Liebes! Wie geht es dir?" fragt sie.

"Gut, Schwester", sagt Zelda. "Wie geht es dir?"

"Toll! Ich habe eine großartige Idee", sagt Yolanda. "**Wir sollten** zusammen verreisen!"

"Was für eine tolle Idee", sagt Zelda. "**Ich liebe** sie! Wohin?"

"Ich weiß nicht, irgendwo", sagt Yolanda. "Wo auch immer! **Ich würde** mit dir überall hingehen!"

"Lass uns morgen ins Reisebüro gehen", sagt Zelda. "Die können helfen."

Die Schwestern treffen sich am nächsten Tag. Zelda bringt Broschüren mit Ideen für Urlaubsreisen mit. Die Broschüren bieten verschiedene Arten des Tourismus an. Es gibt

Erholungsreisen, wie Entspannung und Spaß am Strand. Es gibt Kulturreisen wie Sightseeing oder Museumsbesuche, um mehr über Geschichte und Kunst zu erfahren. Abenteuerreisen sind für Menschen, **die es lieben**, ferne Orte zu erkunden und Extremsportarten auszuüben. Ökotourismus ist eine auf die Belange von Umwelt und ansässiger Bevölkerung besondere Rücksicht nehmende Form des Tourismus.

Yolanda liest die Zeitungen. Gesundheitstourismus ist Reisen zur Pflege von Körper und Geist durch den Besuch von Orten wie Kurorten. Religiöser Tourismus ist Reisen, um religiöse Veranstaltungen oder wichtige religiöse Orte zu besuchen.

"Es gibt so viele Arten von Reisen", sagt Yolanda.

"Ja", sagt Zelda. "**Ich** reise **gerne** aus einem bestimmten Grund. Ich kann es nicht ertragen, am Strand zu liegen und nichts zu tun." Yolanda mag den Strand. Sie macht gerne nichts im Urlaub, sie sagt nichts.

Die Schwestern kommen im Reisebüro an. Der Reiseanbieter ist eine Frau. Sie scheint nett zu sein. Yolanda und Zelda setzen sich mit ihr hin.

"Wie kann ich Ihnen helfen?" fragt die Reiseanbieterin.

"Wir würden gerne verreisen", sagt Yolanda.

"Was für eine Reise?" fragt die Reiseanbieterin.

"**Ich bin verrückt nach** Kultur", sagt Zelda. "Ich liebe Museen, ich liebe Kunst."

"**Ich würde lieber** irgendwo hingehen, wo die Sonnen scheint. Ich liebe Außenaktivitäten", sagt Yolanda.

"Menschen reisen aus vielen Gründen", sagt die Reiseanbieterin. "Wie wäre es mit Barcelona?"

"Oh, ich weiß nicht", sagt Zelda. "**Ich kann es nicht ertragen**, die Landessprache nicht zu kennen."

"Wir sprechen kein Spanisch", sagt Yolanda.

"Würde Ihnen Paris gefallen?" fragt die Reiseanbieterin. "Es gibt dort sehr gute Museen und Restaurants."

"Wir sprechen auch kein Französisch", sagen sie beide.

"Wie wäre es mit London?" fragt die Reiseanbieterin.

"Toll!" sagt Zelda.

"So regnerisch!" sagt Yolanda zur gleichen Zeit. Die Schwestern sehen sich gegenseitig an.

"Du hast gesagt, dir ist es egal Yoli", sagt Zelda.

"Ich will mit dir reisen", sagt Yolanda. "**Ich bin nicht sauer wegen** London. **Ich verabscheue** den Regen!"

"Komm schon, Yolanda", sagt Zelda. "Bitte!"

Die Reiseanbieterin zeigt den Frauen Bilder von London. Sie sehen die berühmten Gebäude.

Yolanda möchte Big Ben sehen. Zelda ist begeistert vom Tate Modern Kunstmuseum.

"Was für ein Hotel möchten Sie?" fragt die Reiseanbieterin.

"Wir könnten ein Airbnb nehmen", sagt Yolanda.

"Nein, **ich hasse** es, im Zuhause anderer Leute zu wohnen", sagt Zelda.

"Wir haben schöne Hotels im Zentrum der Stadt", sagt die Reiseanbieterin.

"Das klingt toll", sagt Zelda.

Zelda bevorzugt Luxushotels. Sie weiß, dass Yolanda ausgefallene Hotels **nicht besonders**

mag. Aber Zelda macht nie Urlaub. Sie will, dass dieser Urlaub perfekt wird. Die Reiseanbieterin zeigt den Schwestern Bilder. Die Hotelzimmer sind riesig. Einige haben ein Badewanne in der Mitte des Raumes.

"Die sind wunderschön", sagt Zelda. "Macht es dir was aus, wenn wir in einem schicken Hotel wohnen, Yolanda?"

"**Überhaupt nicht**", sagt Yolanda. Zelda weiß, dass sie schicke Hotels **nicht mag**. Yolanda fühlt sich traurig, Zelda macht, was sie will.

"**Was würden Sie gerne** tun, solange Sie in London sind?" fragt die Reiseanbieterin.

"Wir würden gerne in Museen gehen, den Palast besuchen und einige Kunstgalerien besuchen", sagt Zelda.

"Okay", sagt die Reiseanbieterin, "Das ist wahrscheinlich genug, um Ihre Zeit in London auszuschöpfen."

Yolanda sagt nichts. Die Schwestern zahlen und verlassen das Reisebüro. Zelda ist glücklich, Yolanda wünscht sich der Urlaub wäre mehr nach ihrem Geschmack. Sie geht nach Hause. Sie denkt über die Reise nach. Sie lächelt. Sie hat einen Plan.

Am nächsten Tag kehrt Yolanda zum Reisebüro zurück.

"Hallo, Yolanda", sagt die Reiseanbieterin. "Wie kann ich Ihnen helfen?"

"**Wir wollen** unsere Reise etwas ändern", sagt Yolanda.

"Kein Problem", sagt die Reiseanbieterin.

"**Wir wollen lieber** an einen sonnigen Ort", sagt Yolanda.

"Natürlich", sagt die Reiseanbieterin. Die Reiseanbieterin schlägt viele verschiedene Orte vor. Yolanda unterzeichnet einige neue Papiere. Sie gibt der Reiseanbieterin Geld für die Veränderungen. Sie stellt sich Zelda im Urlaub vor. Sie lächelt. Zelda **mag** Überraschungen.

Es ist Wochenende. Es ist Zeit für Yolandas und Zeldas Urlaub. Die Schwestern treffen sich am Flughafen. Sie sind aufgeregt. Yolanda ist nervös.

"Ich habe dir Kaffee gebracht", sagt sie. Zelda nimmt den Kaffee.

"Danke", sagt sie. Sie trinkt einen Schluck. "Oh, aber **ich hasse** Zucker in meinem Kaffee, Yoli!"

Yolanda entschuldigt sich. Sie nimmt beide Kaffees in die Hände. Jetzt kann sie ihren Koffer nicht tragen.

Die beiden Schwestern gehen durch die Sicherheitskontrolle. Sie warten, bis sie an Bord des Flugzeugs können. Auf dem Bildschirm steht "Flug 361 nach London / mit Anschlussflug / British Airways". Yolanda lächelt, als sie ins Flugzeug steigen.

Der Flug dauert sechs Stunden. Yolanda und Zelda schlafen. Sie wachen auf, als das Flugzeug auf dem Flughafen in London eintrifft. Die Flugbegleiterin benutzt den Lautsprecher. "Wenn Sie in London bleiben oder einen Weiterflug haben, verlassen Sie bitte das Flugzeug."

Zelda steht auf. Yolanda nicht.

"Komm schon, Yolanda", sagt Zelda. Yolanda bewegt sich nicht.

"Gehen wir!" sagt Zelda.

"Eigentlich, Schwester", sagt Yolanda, "Es gibt eine Planänderung. Wir bleiben in diesem Flugzeug."

Zelda sieht verwirrt aus.

Die Flugbegleiterin benutzt wieder den Lautsprecher: "Wenn Sie zu unserem nächsten Ziel reisen, bleiben Sie auf Ihren Plätzen. Nächster Halt - Fidschi!"

ZUSAMMENFASSUNG

Zwei Schwestern, Yolanda und Zelda, wollen zusammen verreisen. Sie gehen zum Reisebüro. Sie sind sehr verschieden. Es ist schwierig für sie, sich auf einen Ort zu einigen. Zelda mag es Kunst und Kultur zu sehen. Yolanda bevorzugt es am Strand zu liegen. Schließlich entscheiden sie, wohin sie gehen möchten. Aber am nächsten Tag kehrt Yolanda zum Reisebüro zurück. Sie ändert das Ziel. Zelda erfährt es, wenn ihr Flugzeug landet.

VOKABELLISTE

Wir sollten	we should
Ich liebe	I love
Ich würde	I would
Ich liebe es	I adore
Ich genieße es	I enjoy
Ich kann es nicht ertragen	I can't stand
wir möchten gerne	we would like
Ich bin verrückt nach	I'm crazy about
Ich ziehe es vor	I prefer
Ich ertrage es nicht	I can't bear
würdest du gerne	would you like
Ich bin nicht sauer	I'm not mad about
Ich verabscheue	I detest
Ich hasse	I loathe

nicht mögen	doesn't like
besonders	very much
überhaupt nicht	not at all
nicht mögen	dislikes
was würden sie gerne	what would you like
wir wollen	we want
wir würden lieber	we would rather
mögen	likes
Ich hasse	I hate

FRAGEN

1) Woher kennen sich Yolanda und Zelda?

    a) sie sind Freunde

b) sie sind Schwestern

c) sie arbeiten zusammen

d) sie sind Nachbarn

2) Was macht Zelda gerne im Urlaub?

a) Kunst und Kultur ansehen

b) am Strand liegen

c) sich entspannen

d) was sich ergibt

3) Welche der folgenden Entscheidungen trifft Yolanda beim ersten Treffen mit der Reiseanbieterin?

a) wohin sie gehen

b) wo sie wohnen

c) was sie unternehmen

d) keines der oben genannten

4) Was macht Yolanda, wenn sie zum zweiten Mal zum Reisebüro geht?

    a) fordert ihr Geld zurück

    b) die Reise stornieren

    c) den Bestimmungsort ändern

    d) Zelda anrufen

5) Was passiert, wenn die Schwestern in London landen?

    a) sie gehen in ihr Hotel

    b) sie gehen in ein Museum

    c) das Flugzeug stürzt ab

    d) Yolanda überrascht Zelda mit einem neuen Bestimmungsort

ANTWORTEN

1) Woher kennen sich Yolanda und Zelda?

b) sie sind Schwestern

2) Was macht Zelda gerne im Urlaub?

a) Kunst und Kultur ansehen

3) Welche der folgenden Entscheidungen trifft Yolanda beim ersten Treffen mit der Reiseanbieterin?

d) keiner der oben genannten

4) Was macht Yolanda, wenn sie zum zweiten Mal zum Reisebüro geht?

c) den Bestimmungsort ändern

5) Was passiert, wenn die Schwestern in London landen?

d) Yolanda überrascht Zelda mit einem neuen Bestimmungsort

Translation of the Story

At the Travel Agency

STORY

Yolanda and Zelda are sisters. They have very busy lives. They both live in New York City. Yolanda is a hairdresser for celebrities. Zelda is a lawyer and has two children. They are so busy, sometimes they don't see each other for months.

Yolanda has an idea one day. She calls Zelda.

"Zelda, dear! How are you?" she asks.

"Fine, sis," says Zelda. "How are you?"

"Great! I've had a marvelous idea," says Yolanda. "**We should** take a trip together!"

"What a great idea," says Zelda. "**I love** it! Where to?"

"I don't know, anywhere," says Yolanda. "Wherever! **I would love** to go anywhere with you!"

"Let's go to the travel agency tomorrow," says Zelda. "They can help."

The sisters meet the next day. Zelda brings pages of research on vacations. The pages talk about different types of tourism. There is recreational tourism, like relaxing and having fun at the beach. There's cultural tourism like sightseeing or visiting museums to learn about history and art.

Adventure tourism is for people who **adore** exploring distant places and extreme activities. Ecotourism is traveling to natural environments.

Yolanda reads the papers. Health tourism is travel to look after your body and mind by visiting places like spa resorts. Religious tourism is travel to celebrate religious events or visit important religious places.

"There are so many types of travel," says Yolanda.

"Yes," says Zelda. "**I enjoy** traveling for a reason. I can't stand lying on the beach, doing nothing." Yolanda likes the beach. She likes doing nothing on vacation. She doesn't say anything.

The sisters arrive to the travel agency. The travel agent is a woman. She seems nice. Yolanda and Zelda sit down with her.

"How can I help you?" asks the agent.

"We would like to take a trip," says Yolanda.

"What kind of trip?" asks the agent.

"**I'm crazy about** culture," says Zelda. "I love museums. I love art."

"**I would rather** go somewhere with sunshine. I love outdoor activities," says Yolanda.

"People travel for lots of reasons," says the agent. "How about Barcelona?"

"Oh, I don't know," says Zelda. "**I can't bear** not knowing the local language."

"We don't speak Spanish," says Yolanda.

"Would you like Paris?" asks the agent. "There are very good museums and restaurants."

"We don't speak French, either!" they both say.

"How about London?" asks the agent.

"Great!" says Zelda.

"So rainy!" says Yolanda at the same time. The sisters look at each other.

"You said you don't care Yoli!" says Zelda.

"I want to travel with you," says Yolanda. "**I'm not mad about** London, though. **I detest** the rain!"

"Come on, Yolanda," says Zelda. "Please!"

The agent shows the women pictures of London. They see the famous buildings. Yolanda would like to see Big Ben. Zelda is excited about the Tate Modern art museum.

"What kind of hotel would you like?" asks the agent.

"We could get an Airbnb apartment," says Yolanda.

"No, **I loathe** staying in other people's homes," says Zelda.

"We have beautiful hotels in the center of the city," says the agent.

"That sounds great," says Zelda.

Zelda prefers luxurious hotels. She knows Yolanda **doesn't like** fancy hotels **very much**. But Zelda never goes on vacation. She wants this vacation to be perfect. The travel agent shows the sisters pictures. The hotel rooms are huge. Some have a bath in the middle of the room.

"Those are gorgeous," says Zelda. "Do you mind if we stay in a fancy hotel, Yolanda?"

"**Not at all**," says Yolanda. Zelda knows she **dislikes** fancy hotels. Yolanda feels sad. Zelda does what she wants.

"**What would you like** to do while in London?" asks the travel agent.

"We would love to go to all the museums, visit the Palace, and visit some art galleries," says Zelda.

"Okay," says the travel agent. "That's probably enough to fill your time in London."

Yolanda doesn't say anything. The sisters pay and leave the travel agent. Zelda is happy. Yolanda wishes the vacation was more her style. She goes home. She thinks about the trip. She smiles. She has a plan.

The next day, Yolanda returns to the travel agent.

"Oh hello, Yolanda," says the agent. "How can I help you?"

"**We want** to change our trip a bit," says Yolanda.

"No problem," says the travel agent.

"**We would rather** go to somewhere sunny," says Yolanda.

"Of course," says the travel agent. The travel agent suggests many different locations. Yolanda signs some new papers. She gives the agent money for the change. She imagines Zelda on vacation. She smiles. Zelda **likes** surprises.

It is the weekend. It is time for Yolanda and Zelda's trip. The sisters meet at the airport. They are excited. Yolanda is nervous.

"I brought you coffee," she says. Zelda takes the coffee.

"Thanks," she says. She takes a sip. "Oh, but **I hate** sugar in my coffee, Yoli!"

Yolanda apologizes. She takes both coffees in her hands. Now she can't carry her suitcase.

The two sisters go through security. They wait to board the plane. The screen says "Flight 361 to London / With Connections / British Airways". Yolanda smiles as they get on the plane.

The flight lasts six hours. Yolanda and Zelda sleep. They awake as the plane pulls into the airport in London. The flight attendant uses the speaker. "If you are staying in London or have a connection, please stand and leave the plane."

Zelda stands up. Yolanda does not.

"Come on, Yolanda," says Zelda. Yolanda doesn't move.

"Let's go!" says Zelda.

"Actually, sis," says Yolanda. "There is a change of plans. We are staying on this plane."

Zelda looks confused.

The flight attendant uses the speaker again. "If you are traveling through to our next destination, remain in your seats. Next stop—Fiji!"

CHAPTER 3
Valentine's Day in Paris / prepositions

HANDLUNG

Charles und Dana sind Freund und Freundin. Sie sind verliebt. Charles will etwas Besonderes zum Valentinstag machen. Er lädt Dana nach Paris ein. Paris ist die Stadt der Liebe. Viele Menschen reisen nach Paris, um dort romantische Zeit mit ihrem Partner zu verbringen. Vielleicht sind es die Filme, das Essen oder die schönen Gebäude? Paris wirkt immer romantisch.

Das Paar kommt am 13. Februar in Paris an. Das Flugzeug landet. Sie sind begeistert. Charles und Dana sammeln ihr Gepäck ein.

"Gehen wir ins Hotel", sagt Charles.

"Wie?" fragt Dana.

"Wir können den Zug ins Stadtzentrum nehmen", sagt Charles. **Vor dem** Paar steht ein Schild für den Flughafenzug. Sie folgen den Pfeilen, **unter** ihnen. Sie gehen **über** die Hängebrücke, bis sie zum Eingang des Zuges kommen. Die gehen zum Ticketautomaten.

"Welches Ticket kaufen wir?" fragt Dana. Sie starren beide auf die Maschine.

"Keine Ahnung", sagt Charles. "Das Hotel ist **im** 7. Bezirk." Charles rät, welches Ticket man kaufen soll. Er kauft es und sie gehen zum Bahnsteig. **Oberhalb** der Gleise gibt es ein Schild. Es sagt, wohin jeder Zug fährt. Ein Zug nähert sich. Auf dem Schild steht "centre-ville". Sie steigen **in** den Zug.

Als der Zug das Ziel erreicht, steigen sie **aus** dem Zug aus. Sie steigen die U-Bahn-Treppe hinauf. Sie gehen hinaus. Der Eiffelturm ragt **über** ihnen.

"Es ist wunderschön", sagt Dana.

"Ja, es ist erstaunlich", sagt Charles.

"Ich will **nach** oben", sagt Dana.

"Wusstest du, dass sie alle sieben Jahre den Turm streichen?" fragt Charles. "Mit 50 Tonnen Farbe!"

"Das wusste ich nicht", sagt Dana. Charles erzählt ihr mehr über den Eiffelturm. Er wurde 1889 gebaut. Er ist nach Gustave Eiffel, dem für das Projekt verantwortlichen Architekten, benannt. 41 Jahre lang war es das höchste Bauwerk der Welt. Es gibt viele Nachbildungen des Turms **auf** der ganzen Welt. Es gibt sogar eine Nachbildung in Originalgröße in Tokio.

"Ich liebe Paris", sagt Dana.

"Gehen wir ins Hotel", sagt Charles. Sie gehen zum nahegelegenen Hotel. Es ist direkt **hinter** dem Eiffelturm.

Am nächsten Tag ist Valentinstag. Das Paar hat ein spezielles Mittagessen geplant. Sie gehen ins Restaurant Epicure. Es ist eines der romantischsten Restaurants der Stadt.

"Bist du bereit?" fragt Charles.

"Ja", sagt Dana. "Wie kommen wir dort hin?" Sie gehen **aus** dem Hotel.

"Es ist gleich **hinter** den Champs-Élysées", sagt Charles. Sie gehen die Straße **hinunter**. Sie gehen **in Richtung** des Flusses. Es ist ein schöner Tag. Die Sonne scheint. Dana bemerkt, wie schön die Bauwerke sind. Sie sind alle sehr alt.

"Wir sollten solche Gebäude in Amerika haben", sagt Dana.

"Sie sind älter als Amerika", sagt Charles. Charles und Dana gehen am Fluss **entlang**. Sie halten Händchen. Paris ist eine Stadt für Verliebte.

Epicure liegt **in der Nähe** des zentralen Einkaufsviertels. Sie passieren Geschäfte wie Louis Vuitton und Pierre Hermé. Dana bleibt stehen und schaut in die Fenster. Das Restaurant liegt **neben** einem ihrer Lieblingsgeschäfte.

"Bitte, können wir reingehen", sagt sie. Als sie **durch** die Tür von Hermès gehen, weiß Charles, dass er in Schwierigkeiten ist. Überall sind Handtaschen und Seidentücher. Dana dreht durch. Sie nimmt zwei Seidentücher **von** einer Vitrine. Sie schnappt sich eine Tasche **von** einem Haufen Handtaschen.

"Bitte, Charles?" fragt sie ihn. "Ein kleines Souvenir aus Paris?" Charles denkt nach. Die drei Sachen kosten so viel wie die Flugtickets nach Paris. Allerdings ist Valentinstag. Er ist einverstanden. Dana bringt die Seidentücher und die Handtasche an die Kasse. Charles bezahlt mit seiner Kreditkarte. Sie verlassen das Geschäft. Dana ist überglücklich.

Charles und Dana gehen weiter die Straße runter. Sie sehen das Epicure nicht.

"Es ist genau hier", sagt Charles.

"Wo genau?" fragt Dana.

"Hier", sagt Charles. "Das sagt Google Maps."

"Ich sehe es nicht", sagt Dana.

Charles ruft das Restaurant von seinem Telefon an. "Hallo, wir können das Restaurant nicht finden", sagt er. Er hört zu. Die Person spricht Französisch. "Sprechen Sie Englisch? Nein?" Die Person legt auf.

"Sie sprechen kein Englisch", sagt Charles.

"Es muss hier sein", sagt Dana. Sie entdeckt eine kleine Gasse. Sie geht in die Seitengasse und läuft ein Stück.

"Hier ist es", sagt sie. Das Restaurant ist **in** der Seitengasse, versteckt ganz **am** Ende.

"Gott sei Dank", sagt Charles. "Wir sind schon spät dran!" Sie betreten das Restaurant.

"Haben Sie reserviert?" fragt der Kellner.

"Ja", sagt Charles. "Wir sind etwas spät dran, Charles."

"Folgen Sie mir", sagt der Kellner. Sie folgen dem Kellner. Sie gehen zwischen Tischen mit weißen Tischdecken. Sie sind die ersten Gäste. Das Restaurant ist leer.

"Es ist schön", sagt Dana. Sie sitzen an ihrem Tisch. Es hat frische Blumen **darauf**. Ihr Tisch ist **neben** dem Feuer. Ein goldener Kronleuchter hängt von der Decke.

"Was hätten Sie gerne?" fragt der Kellner.

"Das Huhn mit Pilzen und die Makkaroni mit Gänseleber und Artischocke", sagt Charles.

"Ich empfehle die Makkaroni **vor** dem Huhn", sagt der Kellner.

"Okay", sagt Charles.

"Das Huhn wird mit einem Beilagensalat serviert", sagt der Kellner.

"Perfekt", sagt Charles. "Und bitte bringen Sie uns etwas Champagner." Charles winkt dem Kellner zu.

"Warum zwinkerst du ihm zu?" fragt Dana.

"Das wollte ich nicht!" sagt Charles.

Dana und Charles sind sehr glücklich. Das Restaurant ist eines der besten in Paris. Es hat drei Michelin-Sterne. Der Kellner nähert sich Charles mit den Makkaroni von **hinten**. Sie sind sehr üppig. Sie haben schwarze Trüffel oben drauf. Sie sind sich einig, es sind die besten Makkaroni, die sie je hatten.

Der Kellner rollt einen Wagen zum Tisch. Er hat zwei Gläser, eine Flasche Champagner und eine schwarze Schachtel. Der Kellner öffnet den

Champagner und schenkt ihn Charles und Dana ein. Er lässt die schwarze Schachtel auf dem Tisch.

"Was ist das?" fragt Dana.

"Dana, willst du mich heiraten?" fragt Charles. Er hebt den Deckel der schwarzen Schachtel. **Darunter** befindet sich ein riesiger Diamantring. Er legt ihn an Danas Finger.

"Ja!" ruft Dana.

Paris ist wirklich die Stadt der Liebe.

ZUSAMMENFASSUNG

Charles und Dana sind verliebt. Sie machen zum Valentinstag eine Reise nach Paris. Sie verirren sich bei der Suche nach ihrem Hotel. Sie verstehen die Metro nicht. Weder Charles noch Dana sprechen Französisch. Charles reserviert ein spezielles Essen für den Valentinstag. Dana kann den Geschäften von Paris nicht widerstehen. Sie haben schwierigkeiten das Restaurant zu finden. Dana findet das Restaurant in einer Gasse. Beim Essen hat Charles eine Überraschung für Dana. Was ist es? Ein Zeichen wahrer Liebe. Ein Kellner im Restaurant bringt den Ring mit dem Champagner. Charles bittet Dana, ihn zu heiraten.

VOKABELLISTE

vor	in front of
unter	beneath
über	across
im	in
oberhalb	above
in	into

aus	off
über	above
nach	to
auf	around
hinter	behind
aus	out of
hinter	past
hinunter	down
in Richtung	toward
entlang	along
in der Nähe	near
neben	next to
durch	through
von	from
von	amongst
in	within

am	at
zwischen	between
darauf	on
neben	beside
vor	before
mit	with
hinter	behind
darunter	below

FRAGEN

1) Wer hatte die Idee, für die Reise nach Paris?

    a) Charles

    b) der Vater von Charles

    c) das Reisebüro

    d) Dana

2) Was sehen Charles und Dana als Erstes in Paris?

    a) der Louvre

    b) die Champs-Élysées

    c) das Hotel

    d) den Eiffelturm

3) Welche andere Stadt der Welt hat einen originalgroßen Eiffelturm?

    a) New York

    b) Tokio

    c) Dubai

    d) Hong Kong

4) Was überzeugt Dana Charles am Valentinstag zu tun?

    a) nach Hause zu gehen

b) ins Museum zu gehen

c) ihr etwas bei Hermes zu kaufen

d) aufhören zu trinken

5) Wie gibt Charles Dana den Verlobungsring?

a) ein Kellner bringt ihn mit dem Champagner

b) er tut ihn in ihr Eis

c) er nimmt ihn aus seiner Tasche

d) er geht auf die Knie

ANTWORTEN

1) Wer hatte die Idee, für die Reise nach Paris?

a) Charles

2) Was sehen Charles und Dana als Erstes in Paris?

d) den Eiffelturm

3) Welche andere Stadt der Welt hat originalgroßen Eiffelturm?

   b) Tokio

4) Was überzeugt Dana Charles am Valentinstag zu tun?

c) ihr etwas bei Hermes zu kaufen

5) Wie gibt Charles Dana den Verlobungsring?

   a) ein Kellner bringt ihn mit dem Champagner

Translation of the Story

Valentine's Day in Paris

STORY

Charles and Dana are boyfriend and girlfriend. They are in love. Charles wants to do something special for Valentine's Day. He invites Dana to Paris. Paris is called the city of love. Many people travel to Paris to spend romantic time with their partner. Maybe it is the movies, the food, the beautiful buildings? Paris always feels romantic.

The couple arrives to Paris on February 13. The plane lands. They are thrilled. Charles and Dana collect their baggage.

"Let's go to the hotel," says Charles.

"How?" asks Dana.

"We can take the train to the city center," says Charles. **In front of** the couple is a sign for the airport train. They follow the arrows, walking **beneath** them. They walk **across** the sky bridge, until they come to the entrance to the train. They go up to the ticket machine.

"Which ticket do we buy?" asks Dana. They both stare at the machine.

"I don't know," says Charles. "The hotel is **in** the 7th arrondissement." Charles guesses which ticket to buy. He buys it and they go to the train platform. **Above** the tracks, there is a sign. It tells where each train is going. A train approaches. The sign says 'centre-ville'. They get **into** the train.

When the train reaches the destination, they get **off** the train. They go up the metro stairs. They step outside. The Eiffel Tower stands **above** them.

"It's beautiful," says Dana.

"Yes, it's amazing," says Charles.

"I want to go **to** the top," says Dana.

"Did you know they paint the tower every seven years?" asks Charles. "With 50 tons of paint!"

"I didn't know that," says Dana. Charles tells her more about the Eiffel Tower. It was built in 1889. It is named after Gustave Eiffel, the architect in charge of the project. For 41 years, it was the tallest structure in the world. There are many replicas of the tower **around** the world. There is even a full-size replica in Tokyo.

"I love Paris," says Dana.

"Let's go to the hotel," says Charles. They walk to the nearby hotel. It is just **behind** the Eiffel Tower.

The next day is Valentine's Day. The couple has a special lunch planned. They go to the restaurant Epicure. It is one of the city's most romantic restaurants.

"Are you ready?" asks Charles.

"Yes," says Dana. "How do we get there?" They walk **out of** the hotel.

"It is just **past** the Champs-Élysées," says Charles. They walk **down** the street. They walk **toward** the river. It is a beautiful day. The sun is shining. Dana notices how beautiful the buildings are. They are all very old.

"We should have buildings like this in America," says Dana.

"They are older than America," says Charles. Charles and Dana walk **along** the river. They hold hands. Paris is a city for lovers.

Epicure is **near** the central shopping district. They pass shops like Louis Vuitton and Pierre Hermé. Dana stops to look in the windows. The restaurant is **next to** one of her favorite shops.

"Please can we go in," she says. When they go **through** the door of Hermes, Charles knows he is in trouble. Purses and scarves are everywhere. Dana goes crazy. She takes two scarves **from** a display. She grabs a bag from **amongst** a pile of purses.

"Please, Charles?" she asks him. "A little Paris souvenir?" Charles thinks. The three items cost the same as the airplane ticket to Paris. It is Valentine's Day, though. He says yes. Dana takes the scarves and the purse to the cash register. Charles pays with his credit card. They leave the shop. Dana is very content.

Charles and Dana continue down the street. They don't see Epicure.

"It is right here," says Charles.

"Right where?" asks Dana.

"Here," says Charles. "That is what Google maps says."

"I don't see it," says Dana.

Charles calls the restaurant on his cell phone. "Hello, we cannot find the restaurant," he says. He listens. The person speaks French. "Do you speak English? No?" The person hangs up.

"They don't speak English," says Charles.

"It has to be here," says Dana. She spots a small alley. She enters the alleyway and walks a bit.

"Here it is," she says. The restaurant is **within** the alleyway, hidden **at** the very end.

"Thank goodness," says Charles. "We are already late!" They enter the restaurant.

"Do you have a reservation?" asks the waiter.

"Yes," says Charles. "We are a bit late. Charles."

"Follow me," says the waiter. They follow the waiter. They walk between tables with white tablecloths. They are the first diners. The restaurant is empty.

"It's beautiful," says Dana. They sit at their table. It has fresh flowers **on** it. Their table is **beside** the fire. A golden chandelier hangs from the ceiling.

"What would you like?" asks the waiter.

"The chicken with mushrooms, and the macaroni with foie gras and artichoke," says Charles.

"I recommend the macaroni **before** the chicken," says the waiter.

"Ok," says Charles.

"The chicken is served with a side salad," says the waiter.

"Perfect," says Charles. "And please bring us some champagne." Charles winks at the waiter.

"Why did you wink at him?" asks Dana.

"I didn't mean to!" says Charles.

Dana and Charles are very happy. The restaurant is one of the best in Paris. It has three Michelin stars. The waiter comes up **behind** Charles with the macaroni. It is very rich. It has black truffle on top. They agree, it is the best macaroni they have ever had.

The waiter rolls a cart to the table. It has two glasses, a bottle of champagne, and a black box. The waiter opens the wine and pours it for Charles and Dana. He leaves the black box on the table.

"What's that?" asks Dana.

"Dana, will you marry me?" asks Charles. He lifts the top of the black box. **Below** is a huge diamond ring. He puts it on Dana's finger.

"Yes!" shouts Dana.

Paris really is the city of love.

CONCLUSION

You did it!

You finished a whole book in a brand new language. That in and of itself is quite the accomplishment, isn't it?

Congratulate yourself on time well spent and a job well done. Now that you've finished the book, you have familiarized yourself with over 500 new vocabulary words, comprehended the heart of 3 short stories, and listened to loads of dialogue unfold, all without going anywhere!

Charlemagne said "To have another language is to possess a second soul." After immersing yourself in this book, you are broadening your horizons and opening a whole new path for yourself.

Have you thought about how much you know now that you did not know before? You've learned everything from how to greet and how to express your emotions to basics like colors and place words. You can tell time and ask question. All without opening a schoolbook. Instead, you've cruised through fun, interesting stories and possibly listened to them as well.

Perhaps before you weren't able to distinguish meaning when you listened to German. If you used the audiobook, we bet you can now pick out meanings and words when you hear someone speaking. Regardless, we are sure you have taken an important step to being more fluent. You are well on your way!

Best of all, you have made the essential step of distinguishing in your mind the idea that most often hinders people studying a new language. By approaching German through our short stories and dialogs, instead of formal lessons with just grammar and vocabulary, you are no longer in the 'learning' mindset. Your approach is much more similar to an osmosis, focused on speaking and using the language, which is the end goal, after all!

So, what's next?

This is just the first of five books, all packed full of short stories and dialogs, covering essential, everyday German that will ensure you master the basics. You can find the rest of the books in the series, as well as a whole host of other resources, at LearnLikeNatives.com. Simply add the book to your library to take the next step in your language learning journey. If you are ever in need of new ideas or direction, refer to our 'Speak Like a Native' eBook, available to you for free at LearnLikeNatives.com, which clearly outlines practical steps you can take to continue learning any language you choose.

We also encourage you to get out into the real world and practice your German. You have a leg up on most beginners, after all—instead of pure textbook learning, you have been absorbing the sound and soul of the language. Do not underestimate the foundation you have built reviewing the chapters of this book. Remember, no one feels 100% confident when they speak with a native speaker in another language.

One of the coolest things about being human is connecting with others. Communicating with someone in their own language is a wonderful gift. Knowing the language turns you into a local and opens up your world. You will see the reward of learning languages for many years to come, so keep that practice up!. Don't let your fears stop you from taking the chance to use your German. Just give it a try, and remember that you will make mistakes. However, these mistakes will teach you so much, so view every single one as a small victory! Learning is growth.

Don't let the quest for learning end here! There is so much you can do to continue the learning process in an organic way, like you did with this book. Add another book from Learn Like a Native to your library. Listen to German talk radio. Watch some of the great German Musical. Put on the latest CD from Sarah Connor. Take cooking lessons in German. Whatever you do, don't stop because every little step you take counts towards learning a new language, culture, and way of communicating.

www.LearnLikeNatives.com

Learn Like a Native is a revolutionary **language education brand** that is taking the linguistic world by storm. Forget boring grammar books that never get you anywhere, Learn Like a Native teaches you languages in a fast and fun way that actually works!

As an international, multichannel, language learning platform, we provide **books, audio guides and eBooks** so that you can acquire the knowledge you need, swiftly and easily.

Our **subject-based learning**, structured around real-world scenarios, builds your conversational muscle and ensures you learn the content most relevant to your requirements. Discover our tools at *LearnLikeNatives.com*.

When it comes to learning languages, we've got you covered!

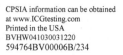